READY-TO-USE

Habit Trackers

*Log daily actions, build healthy routines,
achieve goals and live your best life*

Rachel Watts

Ulysses Press

Dedicated to my husband and daughter, who have both always helped me remember what is most important in life and encouraged me to be the best person I can be.

Published in the United States by:
Ulysses Press
P.O. Box 3440
Berkeley, CA 94703
www.ulyssespress.com

ISBN: 978-1-61243-892-4
Library of Congress Control Number: 2018967983

Printed in the United States by Kingery Printing Company
10 9 8 7 6 5 4 3 2 1

Acquisitions: Bridget Thoreson
Managing editor: Claire Chun
Editor: Shayna Keyles
Proofreader: Renee Rutledge
Front cover design: © Justin Shirley
Cover photos: © Byron J. Watts
Layout: Jake Flaherty

Distributed by Publishers Group West

Contents

Preface

It doesn't seem like long ago that I knew absolutely nothing about myself. Everybody else seemed to know I was disconnected, but I wandered in life aimlessly, trying to figure out what I wanted. My lack of personal awareness led to a lot of awkward situations: teasing, being taken advantage of, and of course, copious amounts of depression and anxiety. As a child, it was really bad. Over time, with friends and an increased understanding of life in general, I started learning more. I learned how to have friends. I learned how to get through school. But, I still relied on people around me for guidance and understanding.

When I was in college, the lack of awareness became a large problem. I was on my own. I couldn't rely on my parents as I had. All of the familiarity, the friends I made... they were all gone.

Once again, I was trying to figure out who I was amid all these people who had it figured out. My depression and anxiety spiked. Things seemed worse than ever. With the help of well-meaning counselors, I waded my way through most of my 20s. I did eventually manage significant progress. I met, dated, then married my husband. We had a beautiful daughter about a year and a half later. Things seemed better until my daughter was 18 months old.

It was like I was back to square one. I wasn't as self-destructive as I had been, but in fear of being that way, I did nothing. My anxiety and depression came back full force.

After finding new counselors and doing work toward improving myself again, it felt like this time, progress was much slower. I kept circling back into the same issues and the same problems, just with different people and different circumstances.

I had a hard time functioning and managing the tasks that most would call "daily life." I'd used paper calendars, digital calendars, lists, sticky notes, and accordion folders in an attempt to bring time and task management into my life. They worked for a short time, but I found myself stuck between maintaining my mental health and the desire to be productive. I felt boxed in by the traditional Type A methods of time management. Until the fateful day my counselor introduced the concept of the Bullet Journal to me.

I immediately fell down the rabbit hole and have been a faithful user for over two years. It's changed my life: It's been a way to improve my time management and productivity. I love the flexibility of the system and that it allows me to take full advantage of my imagination and creativity.

But the Bullet Journal did more than just improve my time management. I started making real progress. At first, I didn't quite understand why, but one of the pivotal pieces of the Bullet Journal is using trackers. One of the primary trackers I relied on was a "habit tracker," which helped me monitor what I was and wasn't doing each month. That habit tracker helped me discover my own patterns and tendencies; things that seemed obvious but to me weren't obvious at all.

I wrote down my moods, my habits, my goals, my sleep patterns... you name it. With the help of the people I loved most, I was able to start objectively identifying key issues in my daily living without feeling an overwhelming sense of guilt.

From there, I continued using my habit trackers and other trackers regularly, and they were so helpful in creating and connecting me with my purpose. They were so pivotal that I got to the point where I wanted to help other people find systems that worked for them, and I launched Planning Mindfully, my signature blog, less than a year later.

Through my blog, I've had the opportunity to get to know many wonderful people and learn even more about myself and other systems that help people succeed. It was amazing to see that so many other people had their own challenges and struggles when it came to time management, productivity, and knowing about who they are and how that affects their journey. Planning Mindfully has received over one million page views in a little over a year. I've been able to quit my full-time job in pursuit of helping people better themselves by managing their life, habits, and time more effectively.

While I'm a huge promoter of Bullet Journals, I recognize that not everybody has the time or patience to create trackers of their very own. Some people create their own tracker notebooks by utilizing printables, stickers, and stencils to help ease the process of creation. This workbook simplifies the process even further. The work of creating trackers has already been done for you, which will help save you time and energy.

Because I feel like personal development is a huge part of the tracker process, I've created a plethora of other pages to help you get more connected with your purpose.

I feel so honored to have the opportunity to help you in your journey to learn more about yourself.

Introduction

Trackers come in all shapes, sizes, and varieties. This workbook will help you find all the ideas you need to set up your habit tracker for success.

Trackers alone do not fix, change, add, or eliminate any of your behaviors.

But learning about how you operate—your patterns, tendencies, habits, struggles, and triumphs—can help you develop better plans to create real change based on your needs and personality.

You may choose to utilize this workbook entirely on your own, for your own personal tracking and data collection needs. Or, you could utilize this workbook with a coach, therapist, teacher, or other important figure in your life to help you improve by understanding how you operate.

How to Use This Workbook

All trackers in this workbook follow either a monthly or yearly format, which will be explained on pages 34 and 35. While there are a few tracker templates in this workbook, you will have the ability to create some of your own trackers to monitor monthly. You may choose to create similar trackers each month, or you may prefer to try different types of trackers month to month.

In addition to tracking habits, you'll also have the opportunity to create personal development goals and use other types of collections and charts.

You'll have a place to organize your information. Additionally, you will personalize your workbook with specific colors and symbols.

While improving your life is a large purpose of this workbook, it is also a means to help you save time and energy. Many people have busy lives and do not necessarily have the time and resources to create trackers for themselves. The majority of this workbook is filled with pre-created structures and trackers—your only job is to start filling them in.

Even if you aren't sure what to track specifically, you have a place with many ideas and suggestions to help you get started.

This workbook is amazing in that it is extraordinarily flexible. It is entirely undated, which means you can start using it at any time you'd like. The other benefit of an undated workbook is if you miss a month, you don't have to waste an entire monthly section to start again! Just flip to the following undated month and begin again. Easy, right?

The other purpose behind this habit tracker's design is to enable you to be as creative as you desire. You can just fill in the trackers as you'd like without using colors and doodles. But the workbook is set up to allow you to have as much fun as you want with your trackers. Color in the fonts. Draw your own doodles. Fill in the doodles provided. Use lots of colors. Try different art mediums, such as markers, pens, and colored pencils.

Using trackers regularly is a lot easier when you get to have fun with what you're creating at the same time.

My hope is this workbook will help you learn more about yourself. You may discover patterns in your tendencies that you'd never realized before! For example, when I use my phone multiple hours a day, I find that I tend to experience more depression and anxiety at the same time.

Use this workbook to discover how you operate, and then use that information to help make you the best person you can possibly be.

CHAPTER 1

What Is a Habit Tracker?

So what exactly is a habit tracker, anyway?

It's pretty straightforward, in all honesty. It's a place to track your habits. Whether you are building new and better habits, getting rid of old bad ones, or simply observing, tracking your behavior over time is a good way to better understand yourself.

Sometimes your habits can be things in your control, like showering, taking medications, and eating junk food. Other times, they can involve activities that aren't necessarily in your control, like having your period or anxiety attacks.

The point of your habit tracker isn't necessarily trying to do what you're tracking in the first place. Rather, it's to help you determine correlations between your actions.

In your habit tracker, you might determine that on the days you don't shower, you're not as productive. In general, this is something you may already be aware of. But with your habit tracker, you're able to get even more specific.

For example, you might discover that on these days, you are much less likely to:

- Take your medications

- Go for a walk

- Get outside

- Socialize with other people

Those correlations aren't necessarily things you would have thought about prior to developing your tracker! In this sense, your habit tracker is the best place to start learning about yourself.

Over time, you can even compare information from your habit trackers with other types of trackers—like mood, exercise, goal-setting, and weather trackers—to determine other patterns with your daily actions. Honestly, the possibilities are endless!

The Origins of Habit Tracking

Habit trackers have been around for a long time in many different forms.

Therapists use habit trackers for their patients to help them learn more about their challenges and tendencies so they can help develop treatment plans to use in therapy.

Parents use habit trackers at home to monitor their children's behaviors and chores. Some teachers use habit tracking with their students to monitor assignments, tests, and grades.

While none of these options are necessarily portrayed as habit trackers, each type of tracker is used for monitoring the regular habits and actions of an individual to help see what is going well or what areas the individual may be having difficulty with.

Ultimately, these trackers help therapists, teachers, parents, and coaches create courses of action for the user to follow that will help utilize their strengths while building upon their weaknesses.

More recently, many people have come to associate habit tracking with Bullet Journals, a creative planning and journaling option that helps you organize your life. In addition to planning your day and journaling your experiences, habit trackers provide the ability to learn about yourself, so you can carry out changes you wish to make in your daily life.

Why Tracking Is So Important for Personal Growth

In many parts of life, we're expected to learn one task before progressing to the next. We can't go to college without going to high school. We can't run before we learn to walk.

Self-improvement is often the same way.

Have you ever tried to fix a problem? For the first week or two, you're generally able to stay strong and steady on the pace of healthy change. Yet, if you're like many, you will inevitably revert to your original habits when something unexpected occurs. You can't pinpoint the exact problem beyond knowing that something is wrong.

If you don't understand your habits, tendencies, and patterns, you'll probably continue the cycle of short-lived improvements for the rest of your life.

Tracking by itself will never fix the problem either, but it does serve as an important grounding step. When you do choose to make progress, you will be able to use the information from your trackers as a means to figuring out solutions that will work better with your personality.

When you get the opportunity to go through your habit tracker at the end of the month, you'll have the chance to ask important questions. Are you doing certain things consistently? Are you not doing specific items at all? Is your activity relatively sporadic?

When you understand your patterns and tendencies, finding solutions to your problems can become quite a bit easier.

While a tracker doesn't necessarily lead to action in itself, knowing your habits and tendencies can serve a huge purpose in your life.

However, there are definitely other benefits of utilizing trackers regularly in your routine.

Trackers are motivating. Tracking can help you continue the pattern of making certain choices in your day. A lot of people mean well when they start a new habit or create a new goal. Unfortunately, most people don't have the means to track this information in their head. That's where trackers come in.

Trackers guide you toward your accomplishments. Using trackers can help you maintain progress.

Those who write down their food consumption tend to have better weight loss. Those who write down their goals tend to reach their goals more often than those who don't.

Trackers help you maintain accuracy. When you write down what you're doing in your daily life, especially right after you complete a task, you're more likely to accurately log information.

Without tracking, people have a tendency to either over-compensate or under-compensate their actions. They may say they ate less than they actually ate, or they exercised more than they actually exercised.

In a way, by keeping a tracker, you're helping yourself to stay more honest and true to your plan and vision.

Can Anybody Use a Habit Tracker?

Yes—habit trackers are for anybody who wants to learn more about themselves!

There's no prerequisite saying you have to have an interesting life to keep a habit tracker. In fact, keeping a habit tracker can help you learn more interesting things about yourself than you give yourself credit for.

Setting one up is actually pretty easy, but sometimes finding ideas to fill them in with is easier said than done.

This workbook will provide you with direction and ideas for any type of tracker you wish to use.

Common Tracking Errors

I've noticed that when people create trackers, they tend to make three critical mistakes that can make tracking much more challenging.

1. They aren't actually interested in tracking what they choose to track.

Have you ever heard the phrase, "You can lead a horse to water, but you can't make him drink it"?

We live in a society that encourages a lot of good habits. We should sleep more. Consider eating less and moving our bodies more than we do. Stand instead of sit. Get better grades. Manage our time better.

And all of those things are great. But if you don't want to create a better habit, what do you think is going to happen?

You aren't going to do it!

When selecting an item you'd like to track, ask yourself if it's something you are *truly* interested in improving or monitoring or tracking. Especially if you're doing this without accountability.

2. The activities being tracked aren't activities they engage in regularly.

Many people have big goals, and I think big goals are great. But if you aren't prepared for working on that goal, you're pretty much wasting your time. A few months ago, I wanted to create a goal of having my daughter use a chore chart every night. But there was a problem with this, since I never even created the chart!

That means the entire month, that goal block sat empty because the chart wasn't prepared.

3. Can you actually achieve what you are trying to track?

It's really easy to dream big. It's a lot harder to achieve those big dreams.

People forget the challenge that comes with adding new habits and goals. I'm not saying that it should be easy to achieve your habits, but is it actually realistic for you to become successful if you don't put in the effort?

How to Build Solid Habits

How does one create a good habit?

Before even starting to track your habits, let's work out how you can create a better routine and mindset so you are better suited toward building habits that you will eventually do automatically.

Get accountability. If you aren't using this workbook with a therapist, coach, or group, consider finding a friend, family member, or colleague who shares a similar interest in bettering themselves, and work together. Bounce ideas off each other and provide accountability for each other if you're having a challenging day.

Start small. People are truly well-intentioned when it comes to starting good habits. In fact, people generally possess a tendency to believe they are capable of doing more than they can sustain regularly.

The point of starting a habit is to commit to a behavior that you can perform regularly. This doesn't mean it has to be difficult! In fact, sometimes if a habit is too difficult, you run the risk of not being able to sustain the habit you're trying to create.

Pair it with other parts of your routine. Trying to commit to a new habit can be challenging if you don't tie it to parts of your existing routine. The best time to add a habit into your day is alongside a habit that you already perform regularly, so it's easier to remember.

For instance, say you want to incorporate meditation into your morning routine. You could add this randomly at any point during your morning, but you run the risk of not being consistent. If you'd like to make this a consistent habit, make a plan to meditate for five minutes after setting up your coffee pot in the morning. Chances are you have to wait that long to get your first cup anyway, so you might as well make that time useful and build your habits.

One way to add tracking into your daily routine is to set up a consistent time and place for using your trackers.

I will fill out my trackers at this time: _____

I will fill out my trackers in this place: _____

Have a backup plan. Having a backup plan can also be useful if your routine lacks consistency, whether it's due to working a job with varied hours, or even if you travel frequently. There are still ways you can maintain consistency even if you can't commit to the exact same time and place every day. Make sure to check out the Tracker Routine on page 45 in the discovery pages to help develop your routine for using your tracker regularly!

Celebrate small wins. If you achieved your goals, celebrate! It doesn't matter whether it's big or small, it's ok to feel proud of what you accomplish. Do something nice for yourself so you feel more motivated to continue making positive choices in your daily routine.

CHAPTER 2

Other Types of Common Trackers

So far, we've mainly talked about habit trackers. There are dozens of other types of trackers that you can build in to your routine as well. You'll find some pre-made for you in this book. If you are drawn to any of the others you learn about in this chapter, you can add them into this workbook using the blank tracker templates.

Trackers tend to serve one of two purposes. They exist either to gather information and data, or to motivate you to continue making positive progress.

Information Trackers

Habit trackers are a type of information-gathering tracker. Other trackers that fall into this category are mood trackers, sleep trackers, time trackers, finance trackers, exercise trackers, gratitude trackers, period trackers, social media trackers, and business trackers.

Mood Tracker

A mood tracker is specifically meant for tracking the emotions you experience on a daily basis.

How you monitor your mood, though, can vary greatly, and there's no one specific way to do this. Mood trackers can be incredibly simple! An example would be a "Year in Pixels" mood tracker. Typically, this type of tracker is done on one page, and you can track your emotions for the *entire year* on this one particular spread. On average, people pick five different emotions and have a corresponding color for each. Then, each day, they color in the emotion they experienced most strongly throughout the day.

Mood trackers can also be more intense and detailed. For instance, you may want to track the levels of five types of emotions daily by rating them on an intensity scale.

You can also have fun, light-hearted trackers for the month. Some people create 30 doodles for the month, and each day, they color in the doodles that correspond with an emotion. Others get more creative with this and may use watercolor so they can use more than one color for each doodle. It's a fun way to show which emotions you experienced throughout the day, but not as intense as rating each individual emotion separately.

Sleep Tracker

A sleep tracker is relatively straightforward and can monitor two things.

When you sleep: While experts recommend adults get seven to nine hours of sleep per night, sometimes this isn't the only important variable when it comes to healthy sleep habits. The other important variable is consistency: are you going to bed and waking up at the same time every night?

How much you sleep: This type of sleep tracker is a bit more basic than the "when you sleep" tracker in that the only element you are tracking is the actual amount you sleep per night.

Sleep is something that we don't get enough of, and people likely don't realize how much sleep they are actually getting per night. Symptoms of sleep deprivation can include depression, anxiety, weight gain, and other things.

In addition to tracking sleep, there are other elements you can include if you'd like to be a little more thorough.

Quality of sleep: How good was your sleep? Did you wake up in the morning feeling refreshed or groggy? You can add a scale to your sleep tracker to determine how good you believe your sleep quality was.

Dreams: Did you dream? While you aren't necessarily writing about your dreams, you can find some interesting patterns in your routine when it comes to dreams. Some people tend to have more dreams during their period, while others recognize that the nights they have dreams, they have poorer sleep quality.

Wake-ups: Did you wake up during the night? How many times? This tracker element can also help you quantify and determine if you're dealing with potential symptoms of a sleeping disorder, which you can later present to a medical professional.

Time Tracker

The time tracker takes the sleep tracker to the next level. Instead of only tracking when you sleep during your day, you actually track all 24 hours of your day, including when you work, spend time on specific activities, socialize, and so much more. The easiest way to do this is to create a 24-hour chart with a key that contains specific colors correlating to specific activities. As you go through your day, you mark your time in with the color of the activities you perform.

Time trackers are powerful tools for helping you see how you spend your time during the day. When people struggle with productivity, one of the first things professionals recommend is to create a "time audit," which is basically managing and tracking how you spend your time each day.

Finance Trackers

The finance tracker can go one of two routes: you can use it to track debt removal, or it can track amount of money saved.

If you're tracking debt removal, you can use a monthly or yearly tracker. Determine how much money you're trying to pay off in a certain time frame. If you choose to do this in a monthly tracker format, you would divide the full amount of the debt by the amount of months you plan on paying off your debt (for example, I want to pay off $5,000 in debt within 12 months, which rounds up to about $417 per month). You would determine in your monthly tracker how much you would pay off per week or per day, and then use your tracker to monitor the amount of money going toward paying off your debt.

In a yearly tracker format, you could dedicate a square within your tracker to represent a certain amount of money. For instance, one square is worth $100 dollars. That means that you need to color in 50 squares to pay off $5,000 worth of debt.

Exercise Trackers

Exercise trackers help you track when you exercise, or how you choose to exercise on any given day.

Simple trackers will only mark off whether you exercised or not. What's nice about a simple tracker such as this is that you could make it part of a monthly goal tracker or part of a yearly tracker.

Complex trackers will not only track whether you exercised, but the duration and type of exercises you performed during a work-out session. The complex exercise tracker would need to be in a monthly format, but it would allow you to get super specific about everything involved with your exercise routine.

Gratitude Trackers

Gratitude trackers typically have a different type of format compared to most trackers. While with most trackers you're ticking off whether you did or did not do something, or very occasionally logging written information, gratitude trackers require you to log longer amounts of information each day. For instance, each day you could complete the sentence, "Today, I was grateful for..."

Monitoring this type of tracker is definitely not as straightforward compared to graph and chart types of trackers, but gratitude trackers can help you improve overall mood and attitude. You'll have these trackers to look back on if you need a positive boost of energy. You also can summarize these trackers in your monthly review, or notice patterns and trends from month to month.

Period Trackers

Sorry guys, this one probably isn't for you. But ladies may find tremendous value in tracking their monthly cycle.

Many women struggle with PMS or a desire to chart for fertility reasons, and tracking your cycle can be positive for monitoring both.

For those who struggle with PMS, tracking periods can help you determine when you start to struggle with symptoms and discover patterns about your body, mood, and tendencies around your period.

Those tracking fertility may be trying to get pregnant or prevent pregnancy. This data can be pivotal for women with fertility issues who struggle to get pregnant. Being able to provide a medical doctor with a detailed tracker such as this could help tremendously in finding the cause of infertility.

It's an easy way to log this critical information in one place. Plus, you can use the data from a period tracker to compare it with other types of trackers to learn more about your body and how it operates.

Social Media Trackers

Are you trying to increase your social media following or improve your engagement? A social media tracker can track elements such as:

- How many people are following you on social media

- How many comments you received

- Your engagement rate

You could actually incorporate many different types of social media within one tracker, too. You could track Instagram, Facebook, Pinterest, LinkedIn, Twitter, or any other types of social media you use regularly.

Business Trackers

Running a business or serving as a manager can be tough work with a lot of small details to remember regularly. If you run your own business, a business tracker can help you monitor aspects of your business, such as:

- How many clients you are working with at any one given time

- Monthly income

- Monthly expenses

- Page views for blogs and websites

- Sales of specific products

Progress Trackers

The trackers in this category tend to be very action driven. When you use a progress-oriented tracker, you intend to complete certain objectives or reach certain goals every day. These types of trackers will help you complete tasks and achieve goals more steadily, instead of just providing general information.

Chore Trackers

For some people, the thought of completing all their tasks on their checklist is oh so satisfying! Thus, having a tracking chart for your chores would be a perfect addition to add to this workbook.

Write out which chores need to be completed on a daily, weekly, and monthly basis and make sure to check them off. The more you check off, the cleaner your house should be, too!

Health Trackers

Health trackers help you improve your health by tracking more general aspects of your exercise and food consumption. While they don't get super specific, a general health tracker can help motivate you to check off the boxes each day by making positive choices in regard to your health.

Goal Trackers

Goal trackers actually are very similar to habit trackers in how you monitor and track your information. However, the primary difference between a goal tracker and a habit tracker is that you are actively trying achieve the goals you are tracking, rather than just observing patterns and tendencies in your daily routine.

You may find that some trackers can both help you gather information about yourself and serve as a motivator to continue making progress at the same time.

Miscellaneous Trackers

Miscellaneous trackers revolve around one-time or seasonal events and situations. You wouldn't use these types of trackers consistently, but only for the duration of time you're working toward something.

They can help you monitor your progress toward completion, track what tasks still need to be finished, and provide a timeline of sorts to help you finish your task fully and on time.

Miscellaneous trackers include holiday trackers and special event trackers.

Holiday trackers

A holiday tracker helps monitor events and to-do list items for an upcoming holiday or birthday. This could involve the entire holiday, including the events leading up to it, or it could be to help with preparing for a party, gathering presents, or planning out the day itself.

Special event trackers

A special event may arise that you may not intend to track for the entire duration of this workbook. The point of having flexible trackers is to provide you the ability to change and adjust your needs throughout the year, acknowledging people go through different experiences during that timespan.

Special events could be tracking:

- Running a marathon (training, preparing)

- Creating an event

- Writing a book

- Completing a special project

CHAPTER 3

Using Your Trackers

The monthly trackers in this workbook have mostly been format-ted for you, so you can stick to the basics. In this book, you'll have five pre-structured trackers:

- Habit tracker

- Mood tracker

- Goal tracker

- Time tracker (you may also use this as a sleep tracker)

- Monthly review

Each month also has a blank tracker, so you can choose what you'd like to track during the month. It's up to you whether you want to track the same thing every month, or if you'd rather take the time and try new types of trackers each month.

The yearly tracker is much less formatted. You can choose how you want to fill it out.

How to Use a Tracker

Using a tracker can be as simple as starting to log what you want to track, and then tracking those items daily.

But to be successful long term with using a tracker, you should create a plan of action for how you're going to track... and most importantly, why you're tracking.

Chapter 5 is filled with pages that will provide guidance in learning more about where you are at and what you want to accomplish. You will use the vision tools as a means of discovering what goals you'd like to achieve over the course of the next year.

You'll also be able to use the Key on page 61 to help organize your information.

Keys help to keep your tracking consistent from month to month. Certain colors may correspond with certain pieces of information, such as yellow representing happiness, and red representing anger.

Beyond colors, you can also use simple doodles and shapes to represent specific information. For example, an "X" in a tracker box could mean that you didn't use the tracker for the day.

Maintaining consistency with your trackers will help you use them regularly. Not to mention, if you keep the same colors/icons consistent over the duration of the workbook, this will save you time and energy in the long run.

What Habits Should I Track?

The beauty of the habit tracker is you can literally track anything. There are no specific guidelines to follow, there's no set rule saying you need to track a set amount of habits, and you can change them on a monthly or weekly basis.

Yet, sometimes finding ideas is a bit challenging! I've created a comprehensive list of habit tracker ideas to provide some guidance and information on items you can track on a regular basis.

For ease, I've separated ideas into many different categories. You can pick as few or as many from a category as you like.

Personal

Personal habits are those that revolve around your general daily tasks. Here are a handful of ideas you can track for yourself!

Often our personal habits are most strongly affected when other parts of our routines change, so you may want to select quite a few of these ideas to try in your habit tracker.

1. Woke up on time

2. Went to bed on time

3. Took a shower

4. Took medications

5. Ate breakfast

6. Took vitamins

7. No money spent on "extras" (no spend)

8. Read a book

9. No TV

10. Paid bills

11. Took a nap

12. No electronics an hour before bed

13. Prayed

14. Read Bible (or other spirituality books)

15. Kept morning routine

16. Used planner/Bullet Journal

17. Slept eight hours

18. Wrote

19. Brain dump

20. Took pet for a walk/played with pet

21. Journaled

22. Learned something new

23. Practiced an instrument

24. Listened to a podcast

25. Completed goals

26. Tried something new

Relationships

Relationship habit tracking can help you understand how you are spending time with family, friends, and other important people in your life.

You may find value in tracking your relationships if you feel like you're struggling, don't spend enough time with the people you love, or want to improve your relationships.

1. Called family

2. Wrote a letter to a friend

3. Hung out with friends

4. Went on a date

5. Family outing

6. No using cell phone with other people

7. Complimented significant other

8. Sex tracker

9. Went to church

10. Went to support group

11. Did something nice for a friend

12. Volunteered in the community

Social Media (Personal)

You can track social media usage or even communication with others on social media.

1. Limited time on social media

2. Posted on Instagram

3. No social media at work

4. Talked with somebody on Messenger

5. Wrote a nice comment for a friend/family member

Blog

Starting a blog is a lot of work, so you may find value in monitoring your activities. Here are some great examples you can include in your habit tracker.

1. Wrote a new blog post

2. Posted a new blog post

3. Optimized an old blog post

4. Replied to blog comments

5. Replied to social media comments

6. Pinned posts to Pinterest

7. Replied to follower emails

8. Watched educational video

9. Worked on blog course homework

10. Participated in a blogging group

Work

Tracking activities at work are super easy (you could even do these in a Bullet Journal specifically meant for work, too!). When you spend a large amount of time at once place, it's very easy to find common patterns and correlations in behavior.

1. Packed a lunch for work

2. No gossiping with coworkers

3. Received praise

4. Finished a project

5. Cleaned work station

6. Made a certain number of work calls daily

7. Finished to-do list

8. Responded to work emails

9. Went to a meeting

10. Presented at a meeting

Health

Everybody is so health conscious these days that you'll probably want to add at least a few of these essentials in your habit trackers!

1. Ate at a restaurant

2. Ate certain amounts of fruit

3. Ate certain amounts of vegetables

4. Avoided junk food

5. Drank alcohol

6. Ate a certain amount of calories

7. Ate a certain amount of macros (proteins, fats, carbs)

8. Drank a certain amount of water

9. Exercised

10. Went outside

11. Went to the gym

12. Cooked meals at home

13. Took the stairs

14. Parked far away

15. Meditated

16. Did yoga

17. Period

18. Brushed teeth

19. Flossed teeth

20. No cigarettes

21. 10,000 steps

22. Logged food for the day

23. Washed face

24. Used essential oils

Cleaning

Can't remember when you last did a specific chore? Your habit tracker may come to the rescue for your housework!

1. Washed the dishes

2. Made the bed

3. Vacuumed

4. Watered plants

5. Cleared off table

6. Did laundry

7. Put clothes away

8. Wiped off counter

9. Picked clutter off the floor

10. Put trash in the garbage bin

11. Mowed the lawn

12. Shoveled snow

Kids

If you have kids, you can track information about them as well! This can be great when they are going through transitions (such as starting school or potty training) to see if you can find any patterns within their daily behavior.

1. Played with kids

2. Bath night

3. Went to bed on time

4. Potty training

5. No discipline

6. Did their chores

7. Did their homework

8. Read a book before bed

9. Woke up during the night

10. Poop or pee accident

11. Packed lunch for school

12. Playdate

School

See how studious you are by tracking your school activities and assignments.

1. Did my homework

2. Read my textbook

3. Studied for a test

4. Met with a tutor

5. Participated in extracurricular activities

6. Went to all my classes

7. Participated in group discussions

8. Got a good grade on an assignment

9. Had a pop quiz

Personalizing Your Tracker

Depending on the person, some elements from each list could be flipped to other sections. For example, "packing a lunch for work" could be an element of a work tracker, or it could be part of your health tracker.

For your habit tracker, intend to select anywhere from 20 to 30 options to track each month.

If you create specific trackers, plan on adding 5 to 20 items to track and monitor regularly.

Trackers and Collections

What is the difference between trackers and collections? Trackers manage information within a set amount of time. They track a behavior that is performed routinely and/or consistently.

Collections, on the other hand, are typically organized lists that can serve as inspiration or give you the ability to track whether you're doing something on your list. Some collections can even get super specific as to what information you're logging within the system.

To compare trackers and collections, let's use the example of buying presents for holidays.

A holiday present tracker would monitor the people you need to buy presents for, their presents, if you purchased them, and how much each present cost. This is typically done over a specific amount of time, though this is technically a seasonal tracker for most (unless you're one to purchase presents through the entire year, which is always a possibility!).

A holiday present collection would serve as a list of ideas for presents you could purchase or create for each person. This collection is flexible and has no date attached. As soon as some-body mentions something they want, you could write this down on a collection list. You don't have to buy everything mentioned on this list, and this list could be expanded upon and kept for a long, indeterminate amount of time.

CHAPTER 4

After You Fill Out Your Trackers

Once you complete your first few trackers, what do you actually do with this information? You definitely don't want to do all the work to create them, fill them out, and then never use them again, right?

Absolutely not—and that's why each month includes a monthly review section.

Once you've tracked your habits, moods, goals, etc., for at least a month, it's time to start organizing this information and creating summaries of what that information means.

A tracker summary is a written blurb that describes what happened through the last month. This way, if you need to go back and look at information, you're not forced to go through charts every single time. You create clear summaries on what each of your trackers indicate, and then you can put that together to figure out what your patterns and tendencies are.

This summary actually serves as a means to help you make adjustments for the next month.

You don't want to keep tracking the same exact things if nothing is changing, right? Tracking information about yourself is very fluid and your needs will likely change monthly.

For instance, if you've hit a goal consistently for three months, why are you continuing to track that goal? If you want to monitor whether you are still doing it, you can always transition it to your habit tracker. But you may want to start working toward new, different, or even expanded goals for the next month.

Likewise, if you're not hitting a goal consistently (three times per week or less), what's going wrong? Your information screams that your goals and methods aren't quite right. It doesn't mean you have to give up the goal, but this information could indicate that you need to modify or simplify your goal into something a bit more attainable.

What I Include in a Monthly Review

Your monthly review can contain whatever elements you wish, but I tend to follow a specific structure because it's straightforward and helps me meet my needs.

- I have a section for what I learned in my general trackers. In this section, I write down patterns I notice, interesting information I discover, and even things I never realized about how I operate from day to day.

- I have a section for what I learned in my goal tracker. I can write whether I accomplished my goals or not.

- I have a section where I can write what I'd like to change for the next month (add, remove, or modify my trackers/goals). This is probably one of the most useful aspects of the monthly tracker because I have a concrete place to write out my plan for the next month before setting it up.

- I include a section where I can write out what patterns I discovered from the previous month (e.g., I tend to have a bad mood when I eat junk food).

- I like to write out what the best part of the month was, and I also like to write out what my primary struggle of the month was. Sometimes this can help me determine if unusual habits/triggers/patterns were the result of something that happened during the month that usually doesn't happen.

Yearly Trackers

Yearly trackers are the most basic form of tracker because you're compressing 12 months worth of data in one section. A yearly tracker can have a format of 365 grids (year in pixels), or it could follow a weekly or monthly pattern as well (weight log).

Getting to look at a tracker through the course of an entire year can be a great way to discover patterns without having to flip through as many pages or go through each monthly review.

Things you can track in your yearly tracker include:

- Weight

- Mood

- Weather

- Period

- No spend

- Whether you filled out your trackers

CHAPTER 5

Purpose Pages

I highly recommend taking the time to fill this area out before starting your first trackers.

The purpose pages exist to help you understand yourself better. Who are you? What do you want? Where do you want to go in life? Why do you want to improve yourself? Those are all critical questions that can help you determine what you want to track and why.

These pages will help you determine your ultimate goals and figure out what you really want to accomplish. You'll be able to break down your big goals into smaller pieces that you can accomplish sooner, as well.

The purpose pages can also provide reminders throughout the next year as to why you're doing this. If you're feeling disconnected, purposeless, frustrated, or even a little depressed, relying on these pages can be massively helpful in getting back to a positive, productive mood.

Personal Development Plan

Fill out on pages 46–47.

Self-improvement is a wonderful journey, but without a path to follow, you'll find you stumble all over the place. To use this worksheet, rate yourself on where you are at now, what you're good at, what you need to improve on, and where you see yourself after completing the workbook. It will help you determine what is important to you, motivate you to work past the challenging times in life, and remember why you want to accomplish these goals in the first place.

Create Your Tracker Routine

Fill out on page 45.

If you're new to tracking, it's important to figure out how you're going to add this new task to your day. So, you can work on creating a routine directly in the workbook.

This sheet will help you develop a daily plan for filling out your trackers, and even take it a step further by creating a backup plan if you miss a day. There are also some places to write down what you'll do if you stop using your trackers for a while, or if you're away from home or your normal routine.

Vision Map

Fill out on pages 48–49.

Figuring out what you want in life can be a little challenging. The vision map is there to turn your dreams, desires, goals, and visions into something a little more visual. In your vision map, start with yourself in the middle. From there, pick three to six areas where you'd like to see your path grow and improve.

Examples of what you can visualize include:

- Job

- Education

- Family

- Dreams

- Travel

- Health

Then, branch the larger points into even smaller pieces, and continue branching until you have something tangible that you can work with right now.

Level 10 Life

Fill out on pages 50–51.

Part of improving yourself is not just learning where you want to go, but recognizing where you are currently. The Level 10 Life allows you to achieve both at the same time.

In this page, you look at your life in terms of:

- Family/Friends

- Financial

- Career

- Personal

- Spirituality

- Giving

- Fun

- Health

Write out what your best life would look like in each of the eight categories. You can also log what your life looks like currently in each category.

In the tracker, label each section to match up with one of the categories on page 50. Then rate your current position on a scale of 1 to 10 in every category by coloring in the sections of the chart. Over time, you can adjust the tracker.

Long-Term Goal Setting

Fill out on pages 52–55.

The purpose of this page is to help you learn more about what you want to accomplish in life. It doesn't matter if your goals are big or small, realistic or not, whatever you want to accomplish is what matters most in this section.

There are four types of goals that people tend to want to accomplish:

- personal,

- professional,

- family/relationship, and

- financial.

Take 30 to 60 minutes and sit down in a quiet place. If you'd like, you may listen to quiet music, but everything else is turned off. Your goal is to write down *anything* you want to accomplish. No judgements, no "I don't think I can do that." If it comes to your mind and you have the slightest inkling of desire, write it down.

Goal Examples

Personal Goals

Visit the most remote towns, villages, and islands in the world.

Camp in my backyard.

Write a book.

Professional Goals

Start a business.

Graduate from college.

Go back to school.

Get a promotion.

Family/Relationship Goals

Get married.

Go on vacation with family.

Establish a regular date night.

Have kids.

Financial Goals

Make $100,000 per year.

Pay off my mortgage.

Buy a car with cash.

Breaking Down Your Long-Term Goals

Fill out on pages 56–57.

You won't accomplish all of your long-term goals during the course of using this workbook, but you can start working toward them now. The way you can start accomplishing that is to break down your goals into smaller, more manageable chunks.

Select two or three goals from each category (personal, professional, family/relationship, financial) and break them down into manageable steps that you can start accomplishing within the next year. Even if some of the goals are too big to fully accomplish in a year you can create a plan of action that will lead you closer to that goal.

This workbook is approximately 12 months long. Start by thinking of what you can accomplish in one year.

From there, you will break down your one-year goal into quarterly goals. What can you do in three months that will ultimately help you accomplish your goal? Continue breaking down the quarterly goals into monthly, weekly, and possibly daily goals, all while asking yourself what you can do in shorter time frames to help you ultimately hit the primary goal.

SMART Goals

Fill out on pages 58–59.

Now that you've broken down your big goals into small goals that you can accomplish regularly, take time to think about them in a SMART way—make sure they are specific, measurable, achievable, realistic/relevant, and time-bound.

Specific. When you're starting to create your goals, you want to be as specific as possible. You may find using the Six W's to be very useful in helping you get specific.

- Who needs to be involved for me to reach my goal?

- What am I trying to accomplish by reaching this goal?

- When do I need to complete this goal by?

- Where do I need to go to achieve this goal?

- Which things do I need to learn or understand in order to achieve this goal?

- Why do I want to achieve this goal?

Measurable. How will you measure your goal? Your goals should be measurable so you are able to determine whether you've reached your goal.

You can make a goal measurable by assigning values such as numbers or dates:

- I will achieve this goal in approximately 12 months.

- I will achieve this goal when I get 2,000 followers on Instagram.

Achievable. Are you able to achieve this goal? If so, how will you achieve this goal? How realistic is it to achieve this goal?

Goals should stretch you slightly; you don't want what you choose to be easy. By the same token, you need to be able to make sure that you can actually achieve them.

For instance, saying you want to purchase a car with cash in one year may be a bit unrealistic if you don't have money. It may be more realistic to purchase a car in five years, and create smaller goals along the way.

Realistic/Relevant. This step will help you determine whether your goal is achievable. Questions you can answer include:

- Is this the right time to start this goal?

- Does this goal match/work with my other goals?

- Does this goal work with the vision for my future business goals? Family goals?

- Am I the right person to reach this goal?

Time-bound. Goals that are time-bound are much easier to measure. Determining what you can do in certain amounts of time will help you break down what you can do toward achieving your goal. This category will address questions such as:

- When am I able to start this goal?

- What can I accomplish in six months?

- What can I accomplish in one month?

- What can I accomplish today?

Determining what you can do in certain amounts of time will help you break down what you can do toward achieving your goal.

Tracker Routine

I will update my tracker every _____,

before/after I _____.

I will fill out my trackers in this place regularly:

_____

I will work on updating my trackers for _____ minutes.

If there is a change in my schedule and I am unable to keep my tracker routine for the day, I will plan on updating my tracker at

_____ instead.

If I stop my tracker routine, I will start again by:

_____

_____

_____

If I am on vacation or away from home, I will update my trackers by:

_____

_____

_____

Personal Development

What do I hope to accomplish with this book?

Why am I keeping a habit tracker?

I will make using my trackers a habit by...

When I finish this habit tracker, I will...

Plan for _____

What am I good at?

```


```

What do I need to improve?

```


```

What would I like to be better at?

```


```

What skills would I like to have?

```


```

Vision Map

See page 37 for instructions.

Level 10 Life

See page 38 for instructions.

Family and Friends   **Personal**

Career   **Health**

Finances   **Giving**

Fun   **Spirituality**

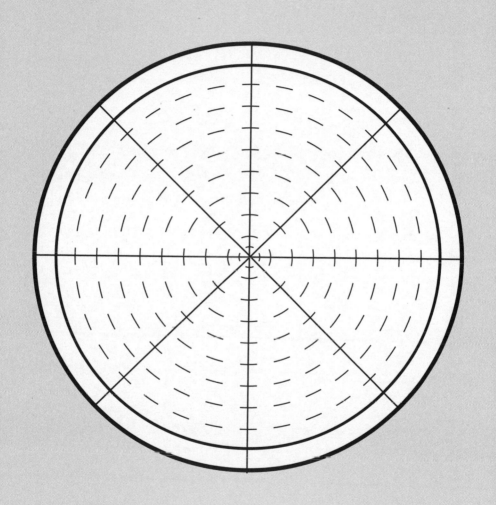

Long-Term Goal Setting

Personal

Long-Term Goal Setting

Professional

Long-Term Goal Setting

Family/Relationship

Long-Term Goal Setting

Financial

Breaking Down Long-Term Goals

Long-term goal...	I can achieve in 12 months...	I can achieve in 3 months...

I can achieve in 1 month...	I can achieve in 1 week...	I can achieve today...

S.M.A.R.T. Goals

Your Goal	Is it SPECIFIC?	Is it MEASURABLE?

Is it ATTAINABLE?	Is it REALISTIC?	Is it TIME-BOUND?

Habit Trackers

Key

See page 25 for how to customize your key.

Goal Tracker

Month

_____

Ready-to-Use Habit Trackers

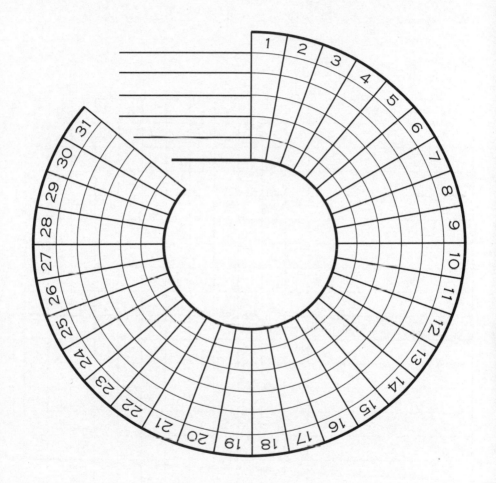

Daily Habit Tracker

HABIT TO TRACK	1	2	3	4	5	6	7	8	9	10	11	12

Month _____

13	14	15	16	17	18	19	20	21	22	23	24	25	26	27	28	29	30	31

Mood Tracker

	1	2	3	4	5	6	7	8	9	10	11	12	13	14	15	16	17	18	19	20	21	22	23	24	25	26	27	28	29	30	31
1																															
2																															
3																															
4																															
5																															

Mood 1 _____

Mood 2 _____

Mood 3 _____

Mood 4 _____

Mood 5 _____

Month _____

Time Tracker

	12	1	2	3	4	5	6	7	8	9	10	11	12	1	2	3	4	5	6	7	8	9	10	11
1																								
2																								
3																								
4																								
5																								
6																								
7																								
8																								
9																								
10																								
11																								
12																								
13																								
14																								
15																								
16																								
17																								
18																								
19																								
20																								
21																								
22																								
23																								
24																								
25																								
26																								
27																								
28																								
29																								
30																								
31																								

Month _____

Ready-to-Use Habit Trackers

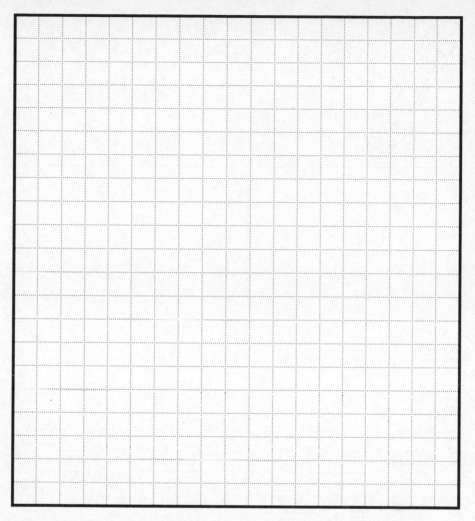

This tracker is for you to fill out however you want! Feel free to structure it the way that works for you, and if you need an idea, try one of these trackers:

- Period Tracker

- Exercise Tracker

- Financial Tracker

- Social Media Tracker

- Business Tracker

Monthly

Review

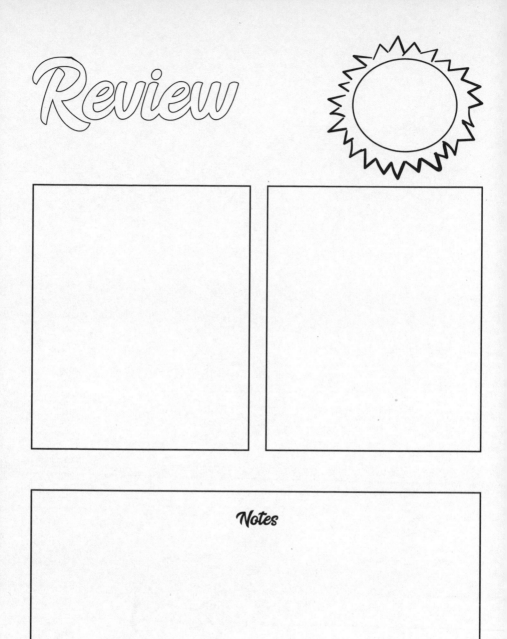

Notes

Goal Tracker

Month

_____

Ready-to-Use Habit Trackers

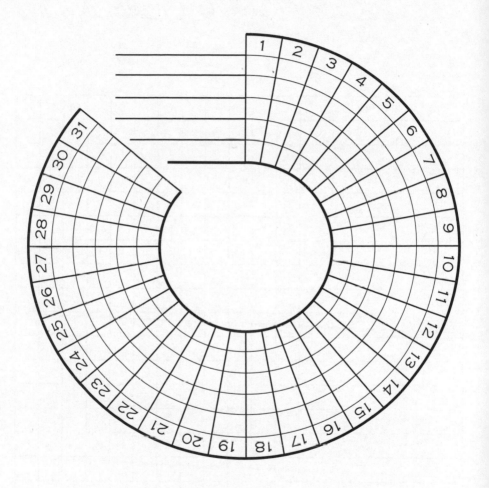

Daily Habit Tracker

HABIT TO TRACK	1	2	3	4	5	6	7	8	9	10	11	12

Month _____

13	14	15	16	17	18	19	20	21	22	23	24	25	26	27	28	29	30	31

Mood Tracker

	1	2	3	4	5	6	7	8	9	10	11	12	13	14	15	16	17	18	19	20	21	22	23	24	25	26	27	28	29	30	31
1																															
2																															
3																															
4																															
5																															

Mood 1 _____

Mood 2 _____

Mood 3 _____

Mood 4 _____

Mood 5 _____

Month _____

Time Tracker

	12	1	2	3	4	5	6	7	8	9	10	11	12	1	2	3	4	5	6	7	8	9	10	11
1																								
2																								
3																								
4																								
5																								
6																								
7																								
8																								
9																								
10																								
11																								
12																								
13																								
14																								
15																								
16																								
17																								
18																								
19																								
20																								
21																								
22																								
23																								
24																								
25																								
26																								
27																								
28																								
29																								
30																								
31																								

Month _____

Ready-to-Use Habit Trackers

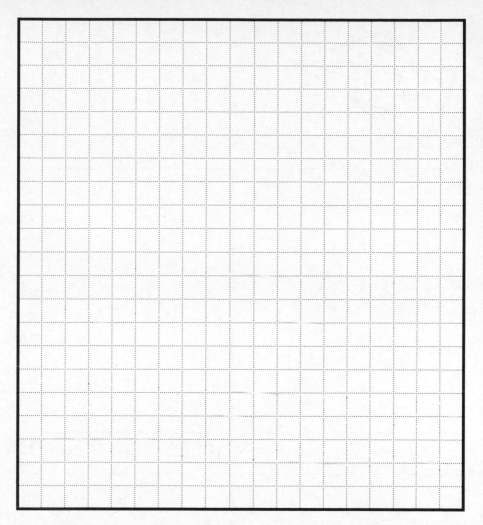

This tracker is for you to fill out however you want! Feel free to structure it the way that works for you, and if you need an idea, try one of these trackers:

- Period Tracker

- Exercise Tracker

- Financial Tracker

- Social Media Tracker

- Business Tracker

Monthly

Ready-to-Use Habit Trackers

Review

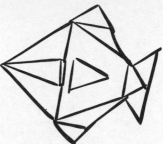

Notes

Goal Tracker

Month

_____

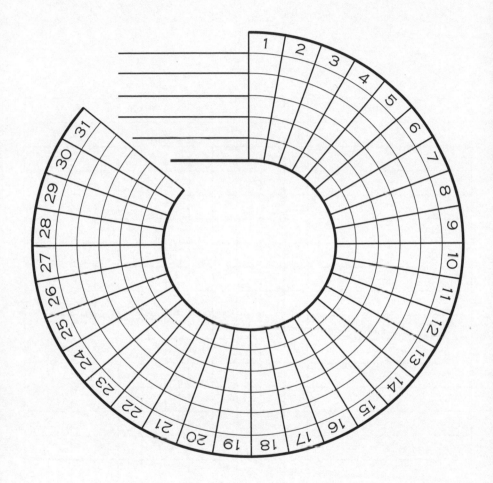

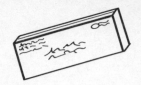

Daily Habit Tracker

HABIT TO TRACK	1	2	3	4	5	6	7	8	9	10	11	12

Month _____

13	14	15	16	17	18	19	20	21	22	23	24	25	26	27	28	29	30	31

Mood Tracker

	1	2	3	4	5	6	7	8	9	10	11	12	13	14	15	16	17	18	19	20	21	22	23	24	25	26	27	28	29	30	31
1																															
2																															
3																															
4																															
5																															

Mood 1 _____

Mood 2 _____

Mood 3 _____

Mood 4 _____

Mood 5 _____

Month _____

Time Tracker

	12	1	2	3	4	5	6	7	8	9	10	11	12	1	2	3	4	5	6	7	8	9	10	11
1																								
2																								
3																								
4																								
5																								
6																								
7																								
8																								
9																								
10																								
11																								
12																								
13																								
14																								
15																								
16																								
17																								
18																								
19																								
20																								
21																								
22																								
23																								
24																								
25																								
26																								
27																								
28																								
29																								
30																								
31																								

Month _____

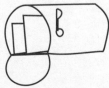

Ready-to-Use Habit Trackers

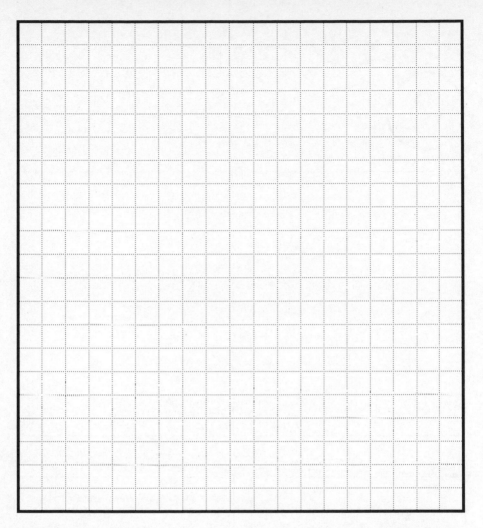

This tracker is for you to fill out however you want! Feel free to structure it the way that works for you, and if you need an idea, try one of these trackers:

- Period Tracker

- Exercise Tracker

- Financial Tracker

- Social Media Tracker

- Business Tracker

Monthly

Ready-to-Use Habit Trackers

Review

Notes

Goal Tracker

Month

_____

Ready-to-Use Habit Trackers

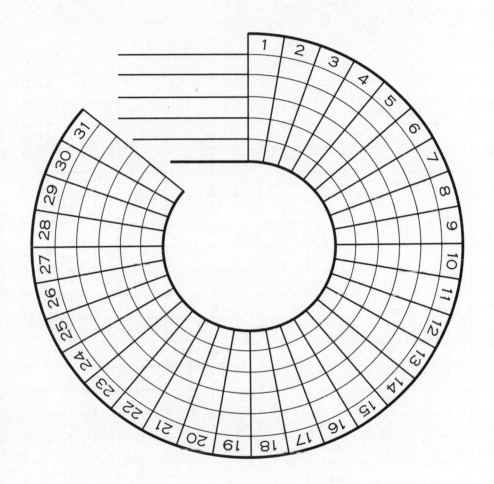

Daily Habit Tracker

HABIT TO TRACK	1	2	3	4	5	6	7	8	9	10	11	12

Month _____

13	14	15	16	17	18	19	20	21	22	23	24	25	26	27	28	29	30	31

Mood Tracker

	1	2	3	4	5	6	7	8	9	10	11	12	13	14	15	16	17	18	19	20	21	22	23	24	25	26	27	28	29	30	31
1																															
2																															
3																															
4																															
5																															

Mood 1 _____

Mood 2 _____

Mood 3 _____

Mood 4 _____

Mood 5 _____

Month _____

Time Tracker

	12	1	2	3	4	5	6	7	8	9	10	11	12	1	2	3	4	5	6	7	8	9	10	11
1																								
2																								
3																								
4																								
5																								
6																								
7																								
8																								
9																								
10																								
11																								
12																								
13																								
14																								
15																								
16																								
17																								
18																								
19																								
20																								
21																								
22																								
23																								
24																								
25																								
26																								
27																								
28																								
29																								
30																								
31																								

Month _____

Ready-to-Use Habit Trackers

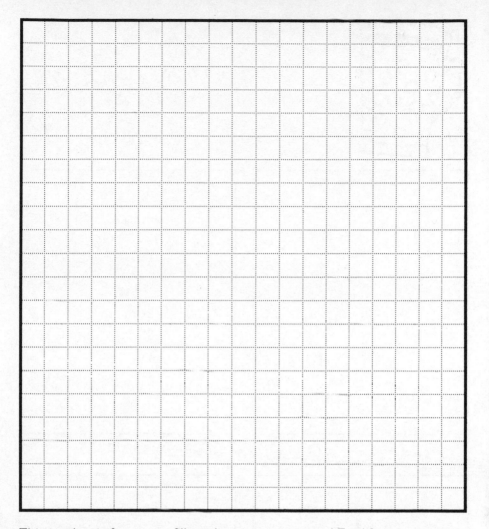

This tracker is for you to fill out however you want! Feel free to structure it the way that works for you, and if you need an idea, try one of these trackers:

- Period Tracker

- Exercise Tracker

- Financial Tracker

- Social Media Tracker

- Business Tracker

Monthly

Review

Notes

Goal Tracker

Month

_____

Ready-to-Use Habit Trackers

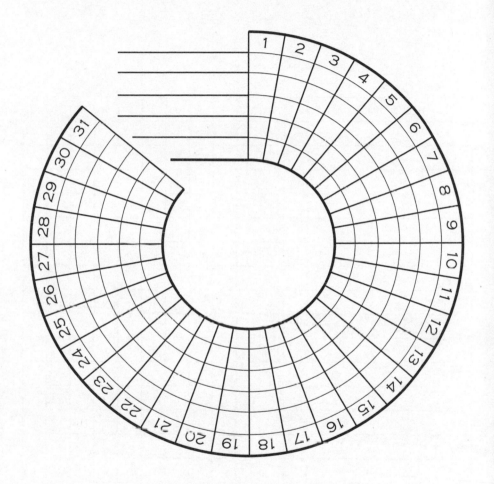

Daily Habit Tracker

HABIT TO TRACK	1	2	3	4	5	6	7	8	9	10	11	12

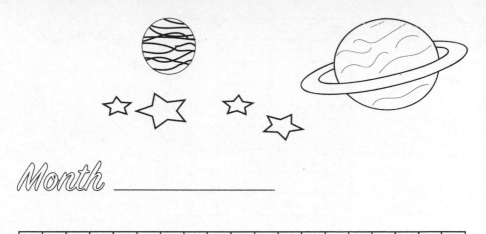

Month _____

13	14	15	16	17	18	19	20	21	22	23	24	25	26	27	28	29	30	31

Mood Tracker

	1	2	3	4	5	6	7	8	9	10	11	12	13	14	15	16	17	18	19	20	21	22	23	24	25	26	27	28	29	30	31
1																															
2																															
3																															
4																															
5																															

Mood 1 _____

Mood 2 _____

Mood 3 _____

Mood 4 _____

Mood 5 _____

Month _____

Time Tracker

	12	1	2	3	4	5	6	7	8	9	10	11	12	1	2	3	4	5	6	7	8	9	10	11
1																								
2																								
3																								
4																								
5																								
6																								
7																								
8																								
9																								
10																								
11																								
12																								
13																								
14																								
15																								
16																								
17																								
18																								
19																								
20																								
21																								
22																								
23																								
24																								
25																								
26																								
27																								
28																								
29																								
30																								
31																								

Month _____

Ready-to-Use Habit Trackers

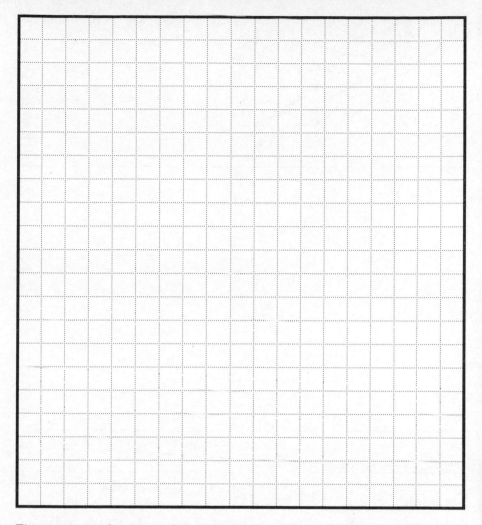

This tracker is for you to fill out however you want! Feel free to structure it the way that works for you, and if you need an idea, try one of these trackers:

- Period Tracker

- Exercise Tracker

- Financial Tracker

- Social Media Tracker

- Business Tracker

Monthly

Ready-to-Use Habit Trackers

Review

Notes

Goal Tracker

Month

_____

Ready-to-Use Habit Trackers

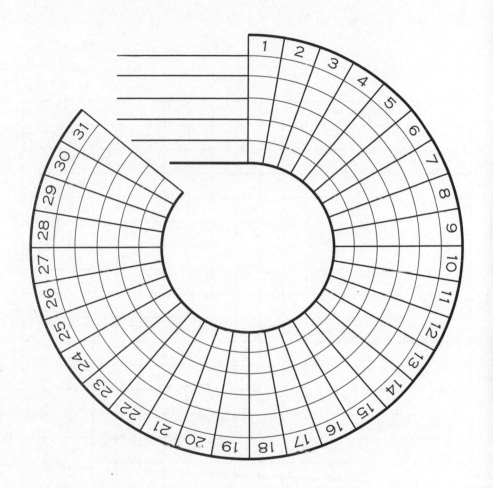

Daily Habit Tracker

HABIT TO TRACK	1	2	3	4	5	6	7	8	9	10	11	12

Month _____

13	14	15	16	17	18	19	20	21	22	23	24	25	26	27	28	29	30	31

Mood Tracker

	1	2	3	4	5	6	7	8	9	10	11	12	13	14	15	16	17	18	19	20	21	22	23	24	25	26	27	28	29	30	31
1																															
2																															
3																															
4																															
5																															

Mood 1 _____

Mood 2 _____

Mood 3 _____

Mood 4 _____

Mood 5 _____

Month _____

Time Tracker

	12	1	2	3	4	5	6	7	8	9	10	11	12	1	2	3	4	5	6	7	8	9	10	11
1																								
2																								
3																								
4																								
5																								
6																								
7																								
8																								
9																								
10																								
11																								
12																								
13																								
14																								
15																								
16																								
17																								
18																								
19																								
20																								
21																								
22																								
23																								
24																								
25																								
26																								
27																								
28																								
29																								
30																								
31																								

Month _____

Ready-to-Use Habit Trackers

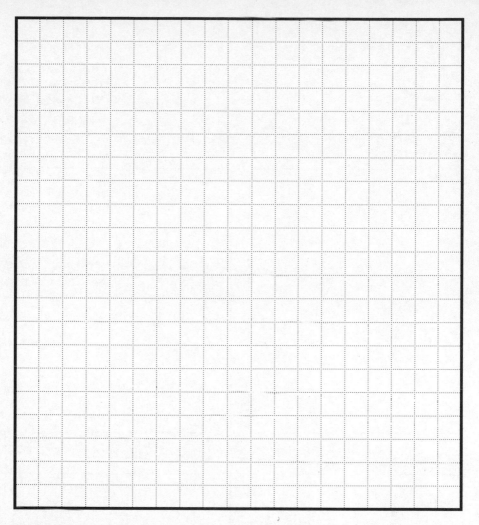

This tracker is for you to fill out however you want! Feel free to structure it the way that works for you, and if you need an idea, try one of these trackers:

- Period Tracker

- Exercise Tracker

- Financial Tracker

- Social Media Tracker

- Business Tracker

Monthly

Ready-to-Use Habit Trackers

Review

Notes

Goal Tracker

Month

_____

Ready-to-Use Habit Trackers

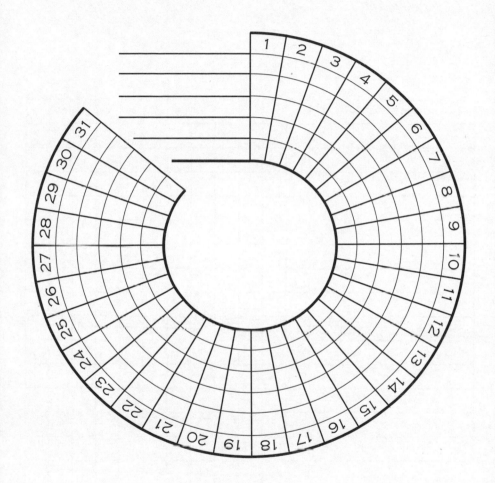

Daily Habit Tracker

HABIT TO TRACK	1	2	3	4	5	6	7	8	9	10	11	12

Month _____

13	14	15	16	17	18	19	20	21	22	23	24	25	26	27	28	29	30	31

Mood Tracker

	1	2	3	4	5	6	7	8	9	10	11	12	13	14	15	16	17	18	19	20	21	22	23	24	25	26	27	28	29	30	31
1																															
2																															
3																															
4																															
5																															

Mood 1 _____

Mood 2 _____

Mood 3 _____

Mood 4 _____

Mood 5 _____

Month _____

Time Tracker

	12	1	2	3	4	5	6	7	8	9	10	11	12	1	2	3	4	5	6	7	8	9	10	11
1																								
2																								
3																								
4																								
5																								
6																								
7																								
8																								
9																								
10																								
11																								
12																								
13																								
14																								
15																								
16																								
17																								
18																								
19																								
20																								
21																								
22																								
23																								
24																								
25																								
26																								
27																								
28																								
29																								
30																								
31																								

Month _____

Month 7

127

Ready-to-Use Habit Trackers

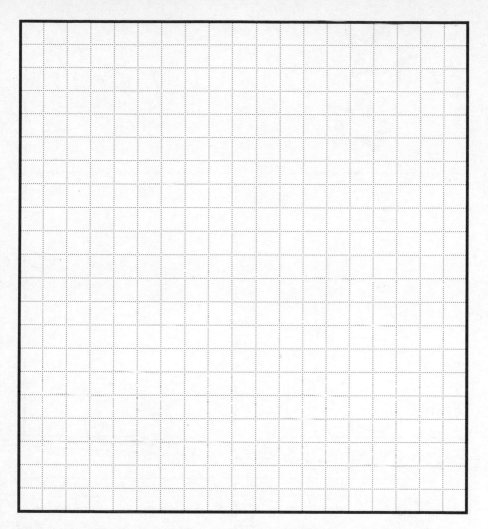

This tracker is for you to fill out however you want! Feel free to structure it the way that works for you, and if you need an idea, try one of these trackers:

- Period Tracker

- Exercise Tracker

- Financial Tracker

- Social Media Tracker

- Business Tracker

Ready-to-Use Habit Trackers

Review

Notes

Goal Tracker

Month

_____

Ready-to-Use Habit Trackers

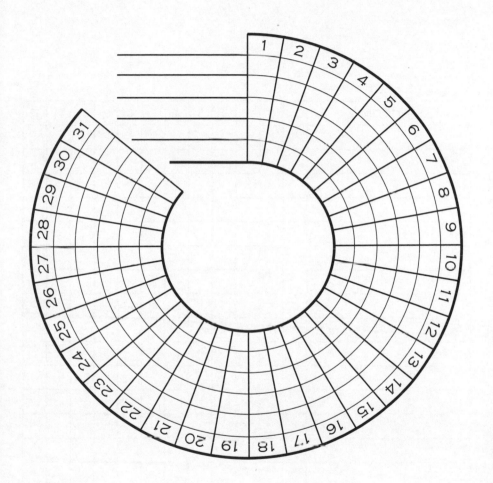

Daily Habit Tracker

HABIT TO TRACK	1	2	3	4	5	6	7	8	9	10	11	12

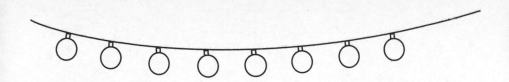

Month _____

13	14	15	16	17	18	19	20	21	22	23	24	25	26	27	28	29	30	31

Mood Tracker

	1	2	3	4	5	6	7	8	9	10	11	12	13	14	15	16	17	18	19	20	21	22	23	24	25	26	27	28	29	30	31
1																															
2																															
3																															
4																															
5																															

Mood 1 _____

Mood 2 _____

Mood 3 _____

Mood 4 _____

Mood 5 _____

Month _____

Let your LIGHT shine

Time Tracker

	12	1	2	3	4	5	6	7	8	9	10	11	12	1	2	3	4	5	6	7	8	9	10	11
1																								
2																								
3																								
4																								
5																								
6																								
7																								
8																								
9																								
10																								
11																								
12																								
13																								
14																								
15																								
16																								
17																								
18																								
19																								
20																								
21																								
22																								
23																								
24																								
25																								
26																								
27																								
28																								
29																								
30																								
31																								

Month _____

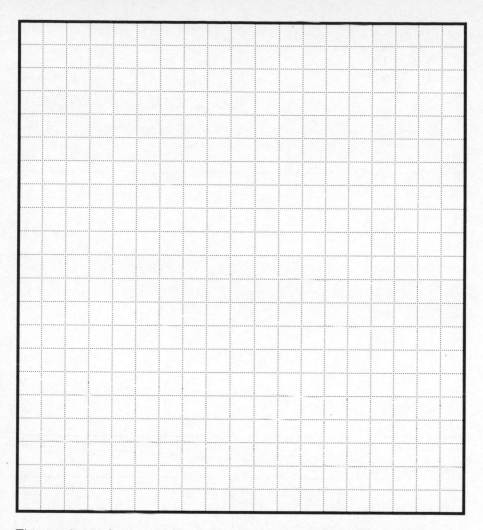

This tracker is for you to fill out however you want! Feel free to structure it the way that works for you, and if you need an idea, try one of these trackers:

- Period Tracker

- Exercise Tracker

- Financial Tracker

- Social Media Tracker

- Business Tracker

Monthly

Ready-to-Use Habit Trackers

Review

Notes

Goal Tracker

Month

_____

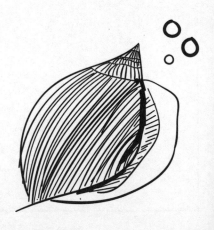

Ready-to-Use Habit Trackers

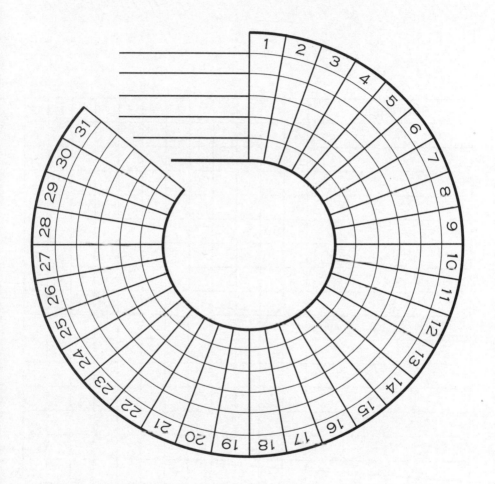

Daily Habit Tracker

HABIT TO TRACK	1	2	3	4	5	6	7	8	9	10	11	12

Month _____

13	14	15	16	17	18	19	20	21	22	23	24	25	26	27	28	29	30	31

Mood Tracker

	1	2	3	4	5	6	7	8	9	10	11	12	13	14	15	16	17	18	19	20	21	22	23	24	25	26	27	28	29	30	31
1																															
2																															
3																															
4																															
5																															

Mood 1 _____

Mood 2 _____

Mood 3 _____

Mood 4 _____

Mood 5 _____

Month _____

Time Tracker

	12	1	2	3	4	5	6	7	8	9	10	11	12	1	2	3	4	5	6	7	8	9	10	11
1																								
2																								
3																								
4																								
5																								
6																								
7																								
8																								
9																								
10																								
11																								
12																								
13																								
14																								
15																								
16																								
17																								
18																								
19																								
20																								
21																								
22																								
23																								
24																								
25																								
26																								
27																								
28																								
29																								
30																								
31																								

Month _____

Ready-to-Use Habit Trackers

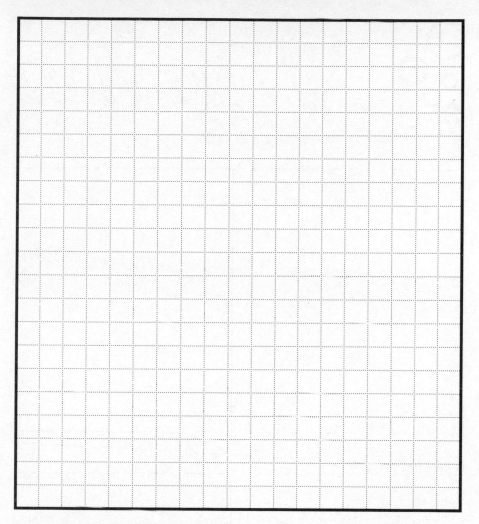

This tracker is for you to fill out however you want! Feel free to structure it the way that works for you, and if you need an idea, try one of these trackers:

- Period Tracker

- Exercise Tracker

- Financial Tracker

- Social Media Tracker

- Business Tracker

Monthly

Ready-to-Use Habit Trackers

Review

Notes

Goal Tracker

Month

_____

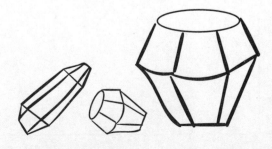

Ready-to-Use Habit Trackers

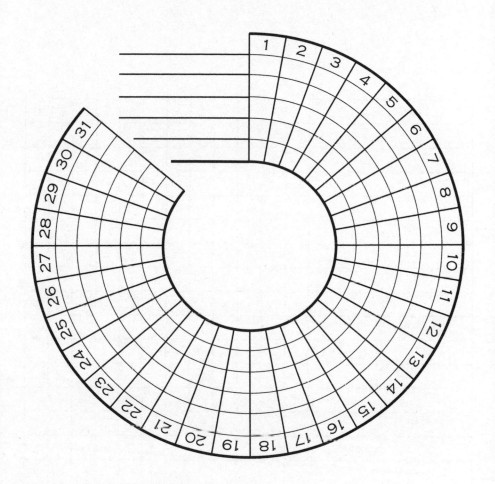

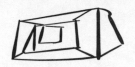 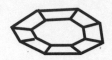

Daily Habit Tracker

HABIT TO TRACK	1	2	3	4	5	6	7	8	9	10	11	12

Month _____

13	14	15	16	17	18	19	20	21	22	23	24	25	26	27	28	29	30	31

Mood Tracker

	1	2	3	4	5	6	7	8	9	10	11	12	13	14	15	16	17	18	19	20	21	22	23	24	25	26	27	28	29	30	31
1																															
2																															
3																															
4																															
5																															

Mood 1 _____

Mood 2 _____

Mood 3 _____

Mood 4 _____

Mood 5 _____

Month _____

Time Tracker

	12	1	2	3	4	5	6	7	8	9	10	11	12	1	2	3	4	5	6	7	8	9	10	11

1
2
3
4
5
6
7
8
9
10
11
12
13
14
15
16
17
18
19
20
21
22
23
24
25
26
27
28
29
30
31

Month _____

Ready-to-Use Habit Trackers

This tracker is for you to fill out however you want! Feel free to structure it the way that works for you, and if you need an idea, try one of these trackers:

- Period Tracker

- Exercise Tracker

- Financial Tracker

- Social Media Tracker

- Business Tracker

Monthly

Ready-to-Use Habit Trackers

Review

Notes

Goal Tracker

Month

_____

Ready-to-Use Habit Trackers

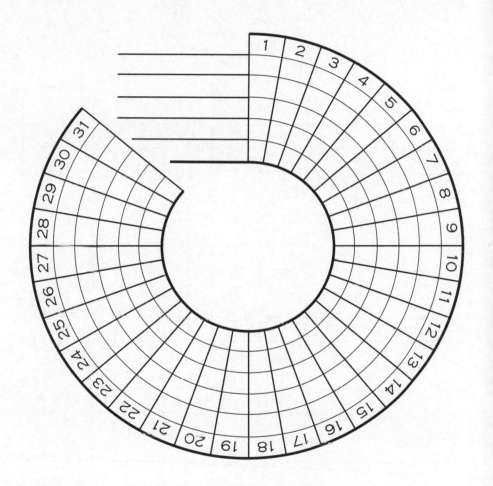

Daily Habit Tracker

HABIT TO TRACK	1	2	3	4	5	6	7	8	9	10	11	12

Month _____

13	14	15	16	17	18	19	20	21	22	23	24	25	26	27	28	29	30	31

Mood Tracker

	1	2	3	4	5	6	7	8	9	10	11	12	13	14	15	16	17	18	19	20	21	22	23	24	25	26	27	28	29	30	31
1																															
2																															
3																															
4																															
5																															

Mood 1 _____

Mood 2 _____

Mood 3 _____

Mood 4 _____

Mood 5 _____

Month _____

Time Tracker

	12	1	2	3	4	5	6	7	8	9	10	11	12	1	2	3	4	5	6	7	8	9	10	11
1																								
2																								
3																								
4																								
5																								
6																								
7																								
8																								
9																								
10																								
11																								
12																								
13																								
14																								
15																								
16																								
17																								
18																								
19																								
20																								
21																								
22																								
23																								
24																								
25																								
26																								
27																								
28																								
29																								
30																								
31																								

Month _____

Ready-to-Use Habit Trackers

This tracker is for you to fill out however you want! Feel free to structure it the way that works for you, and if you need an idea, try one of these trackers:

- Period Tracker

- Exercise Tracker

- Financial Tracker

- Social Media Tracker

- Business Tracker

Monthly

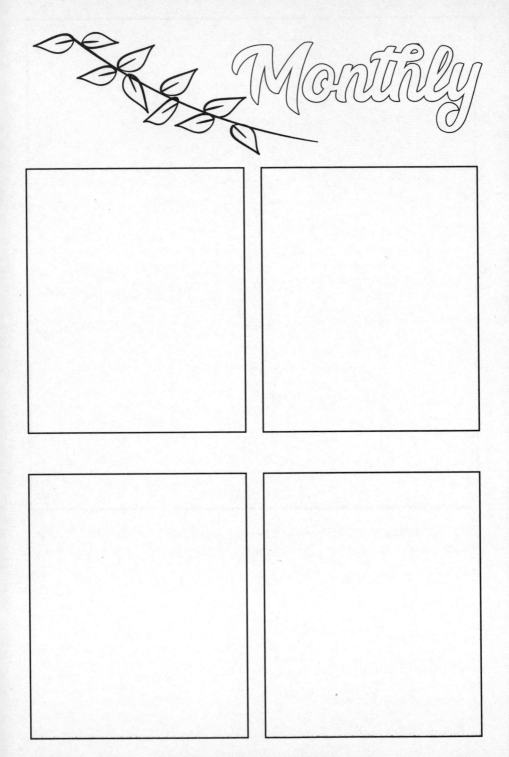

Ready-to-Use Habit Trackers

Review

Notes

Goal Tracker

Month

_____

Ready-to-Use Habit Trackers

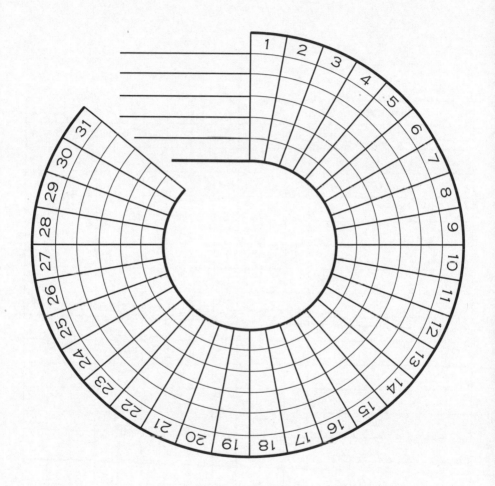

Daily Habit Tracker

HABIT TO TRACK	1	2	3	4	5	6	7	8	9	10	11	12

Month _____

13	14	15	16	17	18	19	20	21	22	23	24	25	26	27	28	29	30	31

Mood Tracker

	1	2	3	4	5	6	7	8	9	10	11	12	13	14	15	16	17	18	19	20	21	22	23	24	25	26	27	28	29	30	31
1																															
2																															
3																															
4																															
5																															

Month _____

Mood 1 _____

Mood 2 _____

Mood 3 _____

Mood 4 _____

Mood 5 _____

Time Tracker

	12	1	2	3	4	5	6	7	8	9	10	11	12	1	2	3	4	5	6	7	8	9	10	11
1																								
2																								
3																								
4																								
5																								
6																								
7																								
8																								
9																								
10																								
11																								
12																								
13																								
14																								
15																								
16																								
17																								
18																								
19																								
20																								
21																								
22																								
23																								
24																								
25																								
26																								
27																								
28																								
29																								
30																								
31																								

Month _____

Ready-to-Use Habit Trackers

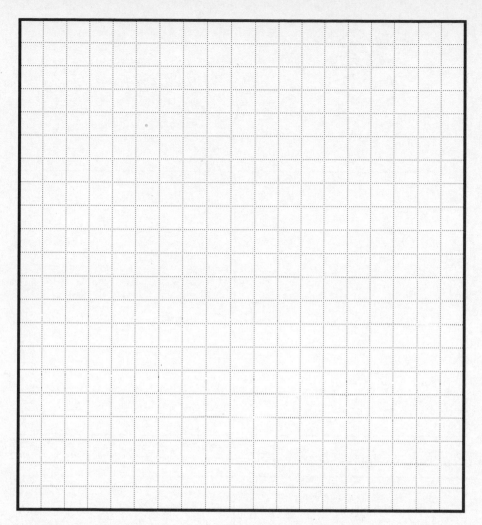

This tracker is for you to fill out however you want! Feel free to structure it the way that works for you, and if you need an idea, try one of these trackers:

- Period Tracker

- Exercise Tracker

- Financial Tracker

- Social Media Tracker

- Business Tracker

Monthly

Ready-to-Use Habit Trackers

Review

Notes

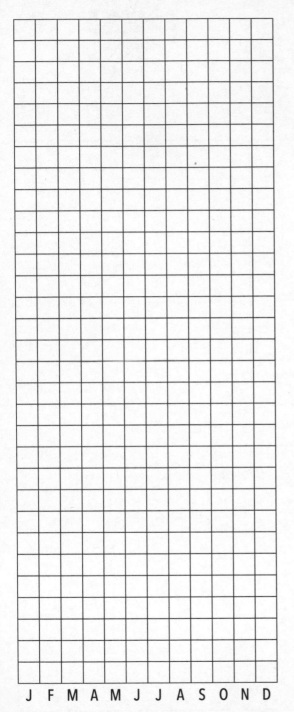

J F M A M J J A S O N D

Yearly Tracker

TYPE OF TRACKER

☐

☐

☐

☐

☐

☐

CHAPTER 6

Troubleshooting

As simple as tracking seems, there are actually a number of problems people run into from month to month. At times, these problems can actually prevent people from tracking regularly and eventually cause them to give up on tracking entirely.

This section will help you work through common issues.

Hopefully, it will also be a relief to know that, yes, it's not just you dealing with this. Even I struggle with my trackers from time to time, and I've learned a lot about troubleshooting and solving problems as I've been tracking.

I forgot to fill out my tracker for a week. HELP!

No worries—life happens! A week or two off is no reason to quit entirely, and there is a reason why this workbook is undated in the first place!

If the empty space is causing you a bit of anxiety, you can try a few things that can help to fill that white space.

- Color in the white space with a dark color; this way, you don't have to worry about accidentally filling in the wrong boxes.

- Doodle in the white space.

- Take notes in the white space.

- Fill in the box with a different color to signify that you didn't track.

In your monthly review section, make sure to note the reason you took a break. Some situations, like emergencies or vacations, are completely understandable reasons for letting your tracker slide for a bit. At the very least, writing it down can serve as a reminder of why you took that time off (it's amazing how much you can forget in such a short amount of time!).

If you took a week off because you forgot/felt overwhelmed/ didn't want to... putting that information in your monthly review can also serve as a way to help make changes for the next month. You can analyze how you dealt with those emotions and create a new plan of action for the next month so hopefully it doesn't happen again.

I stopped using my tracker for a few months. What do I do?

There is no rule saying you have to start completely anew if you end up taking time away. The layout of this workbook is undated specifically for flexibility in situations such as this. You can use some of the principles mentioned in the section above to analyze what caused you to quit for a few months. Otherwise, you can just flip to the next month of the workbook, and start anew.

One of the trackers I've used for the last few months no longer serves my needs. Can I get rid of it and do something else?

Absolutely!

If you're in the middle of the month, you can either doodle or take notes in the white space. Use that space to plan out your tracker for the next month! And while it may be harder, you can also switch the tracker in the middle of the month.

Why am I not reaching my goals?

Have you been trying to start a new goal for a while, but continue to fail? That's ok—it's actually very normal. But, there are a few things you may need to modify to start seeing success again.

Here are some useful questions that may help you understand why your goal is no longer working for you.

Is this goal something you want to do? Something I've noticed when it comes to goal setting is that it's hard to achieve external goals; maybe your supervisor wants you to make a change, or you believe that you need to be a completely different type of person to achieve the results you want in life. If the goal isn't something you truly want to achieve, you're likely not going to make progress.

Can you break it down into smaller steps? Maybe you want to start going to the gym five days a week, but you find that this step is a little challenging. There are multiple ways you can help reach this goal if you determine this is something that is important to you.

One, you could make it a goal to drive to the gym five days a week. Sit in the parking lot, walk into the building, but don't work out. Maybe it sounds a bit ridiculous, but this is a much less overwhelming step and helps you get into the habit of taking yourself there regularly. Once you establish that habit for a few weeks, then consider working out when you go.

Two, reduce the amount of times you attempt the goal. Is five days of gym time unrealistic? Try starting with two.

Is it ok to take a break from tracking for a bit?

Are you going on a fun vacation? Or do you have a family emergency? Are you ill, or going to have surgery? Those are understandable reasons why you would need to stop tracking, though you may still want to bring your trackers with you.

I'd say be realistic. Recognize that if you break your leg, you probably aren't going to run five miles per week. But you still have the opportunity to track other things that happen during your day.

Who knows, maybe you'll find some really valuable information about yourself during those times.

I feel super overwhelmed by my trackers, what do I do?

If you are feeling overwhelmed, you need to simplify. Take out one tracker that you feel isn't serving you well, or even eliminate some of the options for each individual tracker if you don't feel like you can give up any of your trackers. Instead of tracking 20 things, try tracking 10 things instead.

Using all six trackers to start could prove to be challenging initially. Plan to start with three or four tracker types each month. As you master using each one in your daily routine, add another for the next month.

I feel disconnected from my trackers, is this normal?

The most important question to ask is, "What am I hoping to accomplish by using my trackers?"

Did you fill out the pages in the Purpose section (page 36)? If not, I'd highly recommend starting there. If you don't know your "why" behind filling out trackers, it can feel very challenging to continue using them.

I don't feel like my trackers are helping me improve myself. Now what?

Your trackers alone aren't going to be what helps you improve yourself. It's what you do with your trackers that matters.

Have you gone through your Purpose pages? If not, you're seriously missing out. Sometimes creating trackers randomly can make us feel disconnected because we aren't working toward our purpose and goals.

You can also meet with a friend, therapist, or other trusted individual to go over the information in your trackers to look for new information about yourself. As you start to recognize how you tend to operate, it will become easier to find solutions to make positive changes.

I can't use one of the pre-filled trackers because it's not something I'd like to track. Can I choose something else?

Yes, you can! You don't have to follow the pre-populated tracker recommendations. This workbook allows for customized trackers so you have the ability to track what you want to track.

How long does it take to master a habit?

There are a lot of people who say that it takes approximately 21 days to add a good habit in your life. While I'm not certain of the validity of this, make sure to read the "How to Build Solid Habits" section (page 12) for recommendations and tips to improve the likelihood of mastering new habits.

I'm having a difficult time with consistency. How can I improve?

Mind power is very helpful in building better habits, but our brains are very much creatures of habit (no pun intended!). A lot of people don't understand how their actions and their habits correlate, which is a big component of why I have people review their trackers each month to determine what habits/actions/behaviors/moods work together. Review the tips on page 12 to help you with consistency.

Acknowledgments

Thanks to Barbara Hughes, for telling me about the Bullet Journal. Your one small suggestion helped me grow tremendously, not only in bettering myself but helping to establish myself in ways I never could have imagined.

And a big thank you to Bridget, Claire, and the rest of the Ulysses Press team for making this possible and guiding me through the process of writing my first book.

About the Author

Rachel Watts graduated from University of Phoenix in 2011 with a BS in Psychology. She has always had a deep passion for self-help and personality theories and loves to use that to help other people improve their lives. She struggled with time management and organization until her late 20s, when she discovered how powerful habit tracking is. She lives in Rochester, Minnesota with her husband and daughter.

If you would like to get more inspiration in your journey to improve your time management, productivity, and personal development, follow Rachel's blog, *Planning Mindfully*. The purpose of her blog is to help creative people learn to take control of their lives by designing systems that work for their personalities and using tools that best benefit their learning styles. Rachel recognizes that time management and personal development is not a one-size-fits-all journey.